THE 30-DAY OPTIMISM SOLUTION

HOW TO CHANGE FROM PESSIMIST TO OPTIMIST IN 30 DAYS OR LESS

BY: JOHN H. CLARK III

johnclarkbooks.com

Publishing services provided by **Archangel Ink**

ISBN: 1942761562
ISBN-13: 978-1-942761-56-3

Table of Contents

Foreword 1

Introduction 3

Day One...6

Day Two 10

Day Three 13

Day Four.. 16

Day Five.. 19

Day Six 22

Day Seven 26

Day Eight... 29

Day Nine.. 31

Day Ten.. 33

Day Eleven 36

Day Twelve... 38

Day Thirteen 39

Day Fourteen.. 42

Day Fifteen 44

Day Sixteen.. 46

Day Seventeen... 49

Day Eighteen.. 52

Day Nineteen 54

Day Twenty 56

Day Twenty-One 58

Day Twenty-Two... 60

Day Twenty-Three... 62

Day Twenty-Four 64

Day Twenty-Five 66

Day Twenty-Six.. 68

Day Twenty-Seven... 70

Day Twenty-Eight 72

Day Twenty-Nine 74

Day Thirty... 76

Conclusion... 79

Gratitude List 82

Ways to Energize Your Life.. 84

Simple Ways to Relieve Stress:.. 87

Affirmations 90

A Small Favor to Ask.. 93

Get My Books FREE... 94

About the Author.. 95

Foreword

My dear friend, John, asked me to write the foreword to his new book. An honor.

He asked me to discuss, describe, and define the keys to happiness born of the power of positive thinking. As I began to dwell upon this request, a simple thought occurred to me—what sets us apart from all other living creatures is the ability to think and use thought to form decisions, ideas, strategies, and actions.

However, this same "power" can also work against us in the form of small thinking, negativity, depression, or distress. What we see is what we get. How we think is what determines our reality.

I know, I know, we've heard it all before in various ways. Words can be powerful, but words alone cannot change a thing. We have to learn how to view life differently, to see things in different "words." Every day is a brand new day. A new beginning. It is a blank piece of paper on which we get the chance to write a new story.

My problem was that I would always write a story where I was the hero. I have found, over time, that I gain my true strength and happiness by uplifting others. I challenge you to discover and uncover that element of life that you've never seen before, that already exists deep down inside of you. There are 86,400 seconds in a day. Any one of those could change the direction of your life.

Think big thoughts. Grand thoughts. Always dream big. Throw your thoughts and dreams out there, but don't just sit and stare at them. Follow them and pick them up where they land, and then throw them out there again.

If you stay focused and keep repeating the process, you may not achieve your dream in YOUR timing, but when you look back, you will see all the ground you have covered. That is the definition of achievement and success.

The power of positive thinking.

Bobby Field
Entrepreneur, businessman, motivational speaker

Introduction

Pessimism comes easily to me. I come by it naturally. Not quite sure if it is a product of nature or nurture, whether I was born this way or if it is a learned behavior, but I definitely have it.

Most likely, I became a pessimist not so much as a result of genetics—I don't think anyone is born with a negative attitude—but from being around and watching my pessimistic father for the first seventeen years of my life until I went running into the hills. Well, not running into the hills, exactly. I grew up in Houston, Texas, a city built on a swamp near the Gulf of Mexico, so there are no hills. But I did pack my stuff and run to the refuge of a friend's apartment as soon as I graduated from high school.

It was sweet relief, for me and for my family back home. That house was a battleground for a few years, thanks in no small part to my bad attitude.

I maintained, nurtured, and fed my pessimism and negativity over the years, and then several months ago, I embarked on a 30-day self-improvement experiment that centered around alcohol-free living. I decided to go without alcohol for a month and observe what happens, what changes, if any, occurred. I kept a daily log during that month and wrote the results in a book, *Sober in 30 Days*.

I was pleased with how that experiment turned out, and so it seemed a natural follow-up to conduct a similar self-improvement program involving positive thinking. You see, it takes something like 21-28 days to form a new habit. I have the habit of pessimism—looking at the negative side of just about everything. Maybe I can turn that around and replace that mindset with a new habit of optimism—looking at the positive side of just about everything.

So here we go.

I made a list of things I plan to do over the next 30 days to develop a new habit of positive thinking. My other experiment, the alcohol-free one, was designed to break a bad habit, and this one is geared toward forming a new habit.

1. Read a positive message in the morning.
2. Drink one tablespoon of olive oil and one tablespoon of lemon juice (for good health).
3. Post affirmation cards around the house.
4. Practice smiling.
5. Mirror talk—look myself in the eye and say good things about me.
6. Volunteer my time somewhere.
7. Play my guitar every day.
8. Go for long walks.
9. Write every day.
10. Listen to positive thinking CD or deep sleep meditation CD at bedtime.

There are other things, as well—staying off the alcohol, eating healthier, daily meditation—but this is the list I came up with to get things started. It is a list that can be easily modified to fit any situation.

Follow along as I take on this new challenge to change the way I look at the world and hopefully create a whole new me. Well, a better me, at least.

See what worked for me and what did not work. Learn from my mistakes, failures, and successes. Use what you like to design your own positive thinking program. Watch as a regular guy, tired of being a Mr. Negative, works to change his ways.

Like the old saying goes, "If I can do it, anybody can."

Note: *Unless otherwise noted, quotes were located online but an original source could not be identified.*

Day One

> *"Sometimes sand, water, sunshine, and good company are all you really need."*

A new day, a new week, a new way of thinking.

I'm coming off a great weekend in Galveston with two old friends, Bobby and Joe, whom I've known since childhood and who are like brothers to me. Bobby is a gazillionaire and has a beautiful three-story beach house on the west end of the island, a short golf cart ride from the Gulf of Mexico on one side and the smooth waters of the bay on the other side. At night, when you're sitting in the main living room in front of the fireplace and the 52-inch HD television, you can hear the waves crashing against the shore. We played golf at the country club; ate oysters, shrimp, and gumbo; did a little fishing; watched some football on TV; and just generally had a great time.

When we packed it in Sunday afternoon and headed home, I stopped off and met another friend of mine from junior high school, whom I haven't seen since…1972, I guess it was. Craig and I were best friends at one time and ran track together. I was first leg and he was second leg on our district-championship 220-yard relay team in 7th grade.

We were flying high after winning district until we got to the regional meet and they called for our event. When we got out on the track, the other guys lining up to run against us were all at least six-feet tall, with bulging muscles, big Afro hairstyles, sideburns, and beards. Craig and I looked at them, looked at our skinny little selves, and burst out laughing. We slapped each other "five," went to our positions, and proceeded to get blown off the track.

Good times.

Craig told another story I didn't remember at all about the time we were in 8th grade, still running track together, but getting sick of it. Our school was not known for being strong in sports. So we decided to quit in grand style. According to Craig—like I said, I don't remember this—we got cigarettes and a lighter from somewhere, stuck 'em in our shorts, and went out to track practice after school. We were running timed 440-yard sprints that day, he said, and at some point, when we got to the first turn during one of our sprints, we stopped, pulled out our cigarettes, and lit up. Just stood there, puffing away.

Our coach, for some reason, was not impressed. We left practice and never went back.

I reconnected with Craig via Facebook a while back, found out he was living in Galveston, and we finally got together yesterday. It was amazing to be with him again. We've both been through some shit in our lives—mostly all self-inflicted wounds—but he definitely takes the prize for hard times.

Seeing him again was pretty emotional, partly because I had owed him an apology for 40 years. I think it was sometime in 8th grade or maybe 9th grade that Craig and I sort of went different directions, started moving in different circles, and he was being bullied by a new kid at school who had moved in down the street from me. Craig was a little guy, this new kid was an ass, and evidently, it was some pretty serious bullying.

I don't remember any of it, honestly, except for this one time when I was with the new kid and we ran into Craig in the hallway at school. I can still see Craig cowering on the floor, in the corner by an exit door, crying, as Jimmy teased and said I don't know what all to him.

And I stood there and let it happen.

I didn't actively participate, but I didn't stop it. I just stood there and let this jerk pick on my former best friend in the world.

So when we sat down Sunday at a little joint on Seawall Boulevard, we were reminiscing about this and that, and after about five minutes I told Craig I needed to tell him something. I said I wasn't sure if he even remembered, but I wanted to apologize.

He remembered.

And several times during our hour-and-a-half visit, he tried to make me feel better, to ease my guilt and remorse. We could have gone on talking for days, I think, but I had to get on the road to drive four hours back home, and so we walked to our cars, shook hands and hugged, and promised to stay in touch. And I plan to keep that promise.

I'm still kind of processing that whole weekend, I think—from spending time with Bobby and Joe, which always makes me feel better about myself and life in general, to wrapping things up by seeing Craig again. I've known Bobby pretty much all my life—we grew up three blocks apart—and Joe since junior high, but I was never close friends back then with either one of them the way I was with Craig. Bobby and Joe have been best friends forever, and the three of us are really close now, but Craig was my *best friend* at one time the way those two were (and are) best friends.

So it was a strange mix of emotions yesterday. I don't know if it's because I feel like I owe Craig something for not stopping the bullying all those years ago or if there is still some sort of connection. I'm not very good with figuring out emotional stuff.

But the whole thing, the whole weekend, was a very positive experience. I was stressed and distracted most of the day Saturday, but by Sunday—after 24 hours of being around two of the most positive human beings on the planet who love me for whatever reason—I felt noticeably lighter, brighter, and happier. And then I got to see Craig, and that was icing on the cake.

We both have made a lot of bad decisions over the years, done a lot of bad and stupid things. Hurt people; hurt ourselves.

Wasted a lot of years, some would say. But Craig told me that is the wrong way to look at it.

"If you look back with regret, then the rest of your life is going to be miserable. My dad taught me that. Only look back for the good things; don't look back for the bad. You've got to be happy with yourself. I messed up a lot, but I was learning. I'm happy with myself now, and that goes a long way."

"I didn't do everything right, but I didn't do everything wrong, either."

Day Two

> *"I'm learning to love myself, and it's the hardest thing I've ever done."*

Powered up my phone this morning and had a message from Mr. Positive—Bobby. Said he was getting a white chocolate mocha with no whipped cream and no foam from Starbucks, the same drink he gets every morning and the same drink we had before golf on Saturday and before fishing on Sunday in Galveston, and he was thinking of me and wished me well and he had a great time and all that good stuff.

"I hope you have a great week," he said, then caught himself and changed the wish into an affirmation. "I know you will have a great week."

The power of positive thinking.

In the introduction to this book, I listed 10 things I plan to do over the next 30 days to turn myself from a negative thinker into a positive one. Here's what I accomplished today:

I read a bunch of positive affirmations, including the one that headlines today's chapter: "I'm learning to love myself, and it's the hardest thing I've ever done."

Absolutely the hardest thing I've ever done, and for me, the hardest thing I ever will do. Love is such a confusing thing for me, especially loving myself.

I didn't grow up in an overtly loving environment. We didn't say, "I love you," in my house when I was growing up. Ever. It just wasn't done. There was no hugging or kissing, none of that stuff. I never saw my parents express affection for each other. The first time I heard my father tell me, "I love you," was when I was 26 years old. The first time he said, "I'm proud of you," came much later, and that was in a letter that he wrote me. His father never once told him that he loved him, either, even as my grandfather lay on his deathbed. And my dad never told his father he loved him, not even when he knew he was dying. It just wasn't done.

I always felt that my mother loved me, although I don't really remember her saying the actual words. She hugged me sometimes, and she was my mom, you know. Somehow, I just knew she loved me.

So love was a really confusing thing for me. I always thought if I did good enough in sports and in school that my old man would be proud of me and love me—and tell me so. But it never happened. Never happened, despite winning championships, throwing no-hitters, making all-star teams, and earning straight A's on my report card. I guess he just didn't know how to say it.

And loving myself? Who loves themselves? Obnoxious people. Self-centered people. Egomaniacs.

I love myself?

Whatever.

The first time I heard a reasonable explanation of loving oneself and what that really means—or should mean—was during my first walk on the Camino de Santiago pilgrimage in Spain. My friend, Tom, and I were walking one day and happened to meet a young guy named Nick from Manchester, England. Nick was a character, a professional tour guide with the gift of gab.

He had a voice that sounded exactly like John Lennon, and he also possessed a lot of wisdom.

I walked awhile with Nick that day, and we talked about all sort of things, including music, travel, religion, and loving yourself. Nick said that all loving yourself means is that you accept yourself, warts and all, good and bad. If you do the best you can and don't intentionally try to hurt other people, then you're OK. No one is perfect. Even Jesus had his moment of doubt, Nick said.

We're all just human beings, trying to do the best we can. It's OK. I'm OK. Love yourself.

I've heard people say that we should treat ourselves as good as we treat our friends. You don't normally think or say bad things about your friends. You want your friends to be happy. You try to build them up. Why wouldn't you be equally as good to yourself? Treat yourself the same way you treat your best friend.

I also posted a few affirmation cards today in my bathroom. Stuck 'em on the mirror. And I played my guitar for at least 30 minutes. I have a real nice Martin acoustic-electric that I bought a long time ago. Had to wipe quite a bit of dust off of it today. Played a few old songs and worked on some new ones. It's going to take a while to get some calluses back on my fingers.

I wrote quite a bit today, too, and that feels really good. I love to write. Don't like to talk so much, but I love to write. I wish I knew where that comes from, but it's what I'm good at it, and it's something that feeds my soul.

Tomorrow, I get on a plane for Baltimore to visit my wife, who is working out there. We're planning to eat lots of crab cakes and tour Washington, D.C. I'll let you know how it goes …

"Make the rest of your life the best of your life."

Day Three

"Your mind is a powerful thing. When you start to fill it with positive thoughts, your life will start to change."

I think I'm going to like the affirmation cards posted on the bathroom mirror. Posting them there makes it so that one of the first things you see in the morning is a bunch of positive messages. You can't miss 'em. Seeing those every day has to have some sort of effect on the subconscious, I would think.

This is Thanksgiving week, so gratitude is something appropriate to think about today. Appropriate to think about every day, of course, but, hey, we're trying to become more positive and learning to be more grateful is one way to get there.

I refer a lot to my friend, Bobby, and that is because he epitomizes positive thinking. We were at the beach house last weekend, it was early in the morning, and he sat down on the stairs to put on his shoes. As he sat down, he said quietly, to no one in particular, "It's a great day to be alive."

I don't normally think like that, but it's the way he lives. He told me a long time ago that when he wakes up every morning, the first thing he does is say, "Today's going to be a great day." I thought he was kidding, but he wasn't. He really does that. I've tried it myself, and it really does seem to work, but like so many other things that are good for me, I never keep it up for long.

We were playing golf, and I don't remember what was being discussed, but he said, "Hey, you're on the top side of the grass—

it's a great day." Being grateful just for being alive. So simple, but so often taken for granted.

I'm traveling today. I'm a lot better at it than I used to be, but I'm still a nervous traveler. When I went to Spain the first time, I was terrified when I got there and wanted to turn around and come back home, which has always been my reaction when I go anywhere. I got over that anxiety, of course, and I've actually traveled quite a bit in the last few years. But leaving home still makes me nervous.

Today, I got about halfway to the airport—it's a 20-minute drive from where I live—and suddenly I wondered if I'd remembered to close the garage door after I backed the car out. I was pretty sure I hit the remote control button clipped on the visor, but my OCD kicked in and I turned around, drove back home, and checked to make sure. It was closed.

I could feel the anxiety building in my chest as I drove, but I looked at the beautiful clear blue sky and thought about how it was a great day to be alive. And the anxiety lessened. That tightness in my chest started to relax. And I felt lighter inside. Maybe even a little happy.

I've always said it feels strange to me to feel good inside for no reason. Just to wake up and feel good. It doesn't happen very often, and when it does, it's almost an uncomfortable feeling. Like, what is this? What's happening? Where is this coming from? Feeling shitty is more familiar. I'm used to that. I know how that feels. Not that it feels good, mind you, but I'm used to it.

Now I'm sitting at my gate, waiting to board a 12:15 flight in about 30 minutes. This is a small airport and there are a couple dozen people sitting around waiting for the same flight. Everybody is staring at their phone, of course, and I'm staring at my laptop, about to get my phone out and stare at it for a while. But it's good to be alive today. I'm blessed to be able to afford a plane ticket to go spend Thanksgiving with someone who loves me. I've spent Thanksgivings alone before—and Christmases—and that is not a good feeling.

I have a lot to be grateful for, including a job that I hate. If it weren't for that job, I wouldn't have the money, number one, to be sitting here. And even if I did have the money, I'd probably be working today instead of being on vacation. I've been off all week, and that's pretty nice. In three weeks, I'll have another two weeks' vacation. Can't complain about that.

I have a wife who loves me and two daughters who love me, know I love them, and are apparently even proud of their old man, which is very cool. I think that's what I want on my tombstone: *He was a good dad.* That's it.

"There is always something to be thankful for."

Day Four

Today is a day for gratitude—it's Thanksgiving. I'm in Baltimore, Maryland, with the wife, and we're getting ready to drive over to Washington, D.C., and have a look around. How cool is that? I've never seen any of that stuff in person: the White House, Lincoln Memorial, Jefferson Memorial, Washington Monument, Smithsonian.

Life is good, and I have a lot for which to be grateful.

I think number one on the gratitude list would have to be good health. Like so many other things, good health is something so many of us take for granted until it's gone. I've always been blessed with good health, despite the havoc I've tried to wreak on my body over the years. I've had one minor surgery to scoop out some sort of fatty deposit on the back of my neck a few years ago, but no other even remotely serious issues. I remember being at the doctor before that procedure and he asked if I'd ever had any surgeries. I said no, and he said, "Never?"

I am grateful for having a woman who loves me and puts up with me. I know I'm not an easy person to live with. I'm self-centered, moody, and neglectful. But she loves me.

I am grateful for my daughters and for my stepsons. My daughters love me, and my stepsons actually love me, too. They call me Pops. I also have three step-grandsons, and they call me Papa John. Sounds like the pizza chain, but I kinda like it.

I am grateful to still be alive. Quite a few old friends are dead, and I hear now and then about other people I went to school with and such who have died or have serious diseases. I should have and could have been dead on more than one occasion, but I'm still here and still healthy.

I am grateful to have some wonderful friends. I used to ask myself—and sometimes still do—why these outstanding people would want to know me and spend time with me. For what? And the answer is, for nothing. For everything. Probably for the same reasons that I want to know them and spend time with them. I enjoy their company and they make me feel better about myself. I am a better person for knowing them and being around them.

Could it be that I have the same effect on them?

I am grateful for having a good job and career. I've actually had several careers, and I've enjoyed all of them and was good at all of them. After high school, I worked for Brown and Root in Houston as an electrical engineering draftsman, and I became a senior draftsman at age 23, making lots of money and spending every bit of it on drugs and alcohol.

My hobby back then was getting loaded.

As I stumbled and fumbled my way through the rest of my 20-something years, I somehow managed to get a journalism degree from the University of Houston and went to work as a news and sports reporter for newspapers all across the state of Texas. I sobered up during this time, spent fifteen years in journalism, and then became a schoolteacher.

Teaching was great at first, but even though it has become unfulfilling and not something I particularly enjoy any more, it is a good and somewhat meaningful job that has given me other opportunities, including the chance to coach my youngest daughter in basketball and softball for several years, as well as the life-changing opportunity to travel to Spain and walk the Camino de Santiago pilgrimage.

I am grateful for my home. I love the little house on three-quarters of an acre that I share with my wife and my miniature dachshund and lots of tall oak trees. It's peaceful and quiet, and the houses are spread far apart. Sitting here now at the dining room table with my laptop, I look out the window into the backyard and see nothing but grass, flowers, shrubs, and trees.

I am grateful for hope. My life right now is not all I want it to be, but I have hope for the future. I know that if I work hard and believe and think positively, I can make my life into what I want it to be. Not just sit back and dream about what I want it to be, but also put in the work to make it happen.

Or not. Don't do anything and everything stays the same. The choice is mine.

"What's on your mind becomes what's in your life. So think the thoughts you want to see."

- Karen Salmansohn

Day Five

> *"Twenty years from now*
> *you will be more disappointed*
> *by the things that you didn't do*
> *than by the ones you did do.*
> *So throw off the bowlines.*
> *Sail away from the safe harbor.*
> *Catch the trade winds in your sails.*
> *Explore. Dream. Discover."*
>
> - Mark Twain

It looks small when you first see it from a distance, to the side of the Lincoln Memorial and the long Reflecting Pool. A simple stretch of black granite panels set into a grassy hillside, starting with a narrow sliver of stone and growing taller as the panels continue.

I expected something different, more elaborate.

As you get closer, you start to see the etchings, the names, thousands and thousands of names of men and women who died before their time, in war time.

The Vietnam Veterans Memorial on the National Mall, just north of the massive Lincoln Memorial, near 22nd Street and Constitution Avenue. A cold wind is blowing, and it's getting late in the afternoon. The sky is overcast as my wife and I pose for a photo at the head of the pool, with the Washington Monument reflecting in the water behind us.

We look up at the massive Lincoln Memorial, and it is amazing to be standing in this historical place. This is the same place where in August 1963 an estimated 250,000 people gathered and Martin Luther King Jr. delivered his famous "I Have a Dream" speech.

After taking in views of the White House from Pennsylvania Avenue and then also from around the other side, we headed toward the National World War II Memorial and then walked the length of the reflecting pool to find the wall.

With the sky darkening and some nasty looking clouds forming overhead, we decided to get a move on and so we skipped walking up the 56 steps to see Lincoln's statue up close. Aside from the White House, the thing I was most interested in seeing was the Vietnam memorial.

I grew up watching the Vietnam War on television, and I always thought that was my destiny. I can remember as a kid watching the news reports and thinking that when I turned 18 years old, I would be drafted into the Army, get sent to Vietnam, and die. It wasn't a tremendous fear that I remember, really, but just a reality, a fact of life. That's what was going to happen.

I turned 18 in August 1975, two years after the military draft ended. The last American soldier killed in the Vietnam War was Kelton Rena Turner, an 18-year old Marine. He was killed in action on May 15, 1975, two weeks after the evacuation of Saigon, in what became known as the Mayaguez incident.

So I've always been fascinated with the Vietnam War. I always thought I'd end up there. And so the thing I most wanted to visit yesterday in Washington, D.C., was the Vietnam Veterans Wall. It was really something to see.

As we walked along in front of it, I wanted to touch it, but somehow it didn't feel right. Like I was touching something sacred that should not be touched. But curiosity eventually got the best of me, and so I reached out and rubbed my index finger across one of the half-inch tall letters. It was rough, like sandpaper. Then I pressed my hand up against a blank portion of the smooth stone, which felt warm, even though it was 40 degrees, overcast, and windy.

I never knew any soldiers when I was little—my late Uncle Howard was a crew chief during World War II—but I've gotten to know a lot of them since moving to the central Texas area near Fort Hood, and they're pretty amazing people. The thing about it is, they're just regular people who do incredibly brave things.

One time, years ago, I was at Fort Hood interviewing the assistant post commander, a three-star general, I think he was, for a newspaper story. We were sitting in his office, and I told him that his job seemed much like being an executive in a large corporation, except that when his employees go to work, they might die. What is that responsibility like? I asked him.

He didn't flinch. His answer was something like, "My job is to train my soldiers to the best of my ability. If I fail to do that, I should be summarily executed."

That's what he said. And I have no doubt he meant what he said.

We should all be grateful, regardless of the politics and everything else involved in our military, for the people who sign up for such a job.

"Happy people don't necessarily have the best of everything, they just make the best of everything that comes their way."

Day Six

> *"You have to learn a new way to think before you can master a new way to be."*

Flying back home today from Baltimore, an early morning flight that required rolling out of bed before 6 a.m. when it's dark and cold outside, and I almost immediately had to start pushing away the negative voices whining inside my head.

"Ugh, going through security is the worst part about traveling—it's gonna suck."

"Gawd, that was a long two-and-a-half hour flight getting here. Going to be even worse going back."

"Wonder how many times the jerk sitting behind me is going to kick the crap out of my seat."

"Can't wait for the idiot in front of me to slam his seat back into my knees two or three times."

"What's going to happen first—restless leg syndrome kicking in or my butt starting to hurt?"

"Man, I hate flying."

Nice attitude, dude. Good grief…

The difference this time, though, is that I recognized it all as it was happening, and I didn't let my thoughts overwhelm me the way I've always been prone to do. I knew I could just let those thoughts pass on by without giving them the attention they don't deserve. And that's exactly what I did.

No real magic tricks to speak of as I got dressed and got my suitcase packed, sat on the edge of the bed, and drank some coffee. Just refused to give in to the negativity. Like meditation teaches, acknowledge the thought, look at it, and let it slide on past.

Then, when I got outside, I noticed the beautiful, crisp, clear morning. Cold, but not too cold. Listened to some good old songs on the car radio on the way to the airport—Jim Croce, James Taylor, Carole King, Michael Martin Murphy, Beatles, Elton John. My wife and I laughed when we got to the departures area at the Baltimore airport. It was a little congested as you got close, cars coming to a standstill, and people couldn't wait two minutes to get up to the drop-off points outside the terminal building, so they just started parking and bailing out of their cars right there in the middle of the road, doors hanging open, blocking two lanes, popping their trunks, unloading bags, and walking on ahead.

We passed a number of these knuckleheads as the bottleneck opened up and we continued on to the designated passenger drop-off. People are hilarious—the same way they all jump up as soon as the airplane parks at the gate after landing. Everybody springs out of their seat, grabs their bags out of the overhead bin, and then stands there for ten minutes until traffic in the aisle starts moving.

But I digress...

When I walked inside the terminal, instead of having to wait in line to check in, a guy was standing there who took me back out to this little kiosk just outside the front doors and gave me my boarding passes. No mess, no fuss, no waiting. Then I headed for the dreaded security—remove your shoes, empty everything out of your pockets, take your laptop out of the case, run it all through the scanner, blah, blah, blah—and the lines were long, long, long.

I walked up and down, back and forth through the cattle-chute-like pathways until I reached an officer, who promptly shut one gate, opened another, and said, "This way, sir." Ha! Next thing I knew, I was at the front of the line. Didn't have to remove my shoes, empty my pockets, take off my watch or my two necklaces, or pull my laptop out of the case.

So I breezed through security and headed to the gate for my flight. As I'm sitting there waiting, they announce that if anyone is interested in a little extra leg room, there are seats available on the exit row, and due to the plane being full, they are offering to check bags all the way through to final destinations free of charge.

I volunteered for both.

So I wound up not only being able to get rid of one of my carry-on bags—a small rolling suitcase—so I didn't have to drag it through the Dallas airport, but I also had lots of room for my 6-foot-2-inch self to stretch out and be fairly comfortable. I was in the aisle seat and someone else was in the window seat, but the seat between us was empty. Very nice.

So did any of my Negative Nellie thoughts come to pass? Not a one. Well, the clown behind me did manage to jostle my seat a couple of times, but not too bad. Security was a breeze. The flight was quite comfortable. No restless leg syndrome. Butt ache was minimal. And I even managed to sleep on and off pretty much the entire flight.

What is the old adage—90 percent of the things we worry about never actually happen?

Meanwhile, at Dallas Fort Worth International, I was riding a train from one terminal to the next when I remembered that part of this positive thinking program on which I am currently embarked involves learning to smile. I'm not a smiling person, so I plan to work smile practice into my daily routine. Well, as I'm standing in one of the train cars rolling along, I decide to give it a shot and see what happens.

So I do my best to put a smile on my face for at least ten minutes. The train stops, doors open, and people start to get on. A woman steps inside, and I nod at her and she returns a shy smile. Then a man following behind her steps in, and I smile and nod at him. He gives a sort of polite little smile and looks away, then I notice in my peripheral vision that he looks up at me again.

I am still smiling, and this time when he looks away, I see that his smile is a little bigger and brighter.

I'm not exactly a monster—not always, anyway—but to see that kind of reaction from a stranger is a little unusual for me. I'm a big man, and I normally walk around with a not-very-welcoming scowl on my face that causes most people to look the other way.

Apparently, this time, my smile made someone else smile.

"I am committed to being a better person today than I was yesterday. Better thoughts. Better actions. Better decisions."

Day Seven

That simple and brilliant quote was given to me several years ago by an old friend, Sig Christenson, with whom I worked for several years when I was a reporter for the Temple Daily Telegram.

I worked as the only reporter in our Killeen office (Killeen and Temple are the two primary cities in Bell County), and Sig was our city editor. That means he was in charge of the reporters and the daily news production.

Sig used to drive me nuts.

As part of my beat, I also covered the news at Fort Hood, the largest military installation in the country, which sits adjacent to Killeen and is basically the only thing that keeps that city from becoming a ghost town. Well, trying to get news from the military is a challenge, particularly when it involves unflattering news.

After a while, I knew when Fort Hood's public affairs office was not going to tell me anything and not going to comment on certain news events. I wouldn't bother contacting them because I knew it wasn't going to do any good. Inevitably, on those occasions, my phone would ring late in the day, and it would be Sig.

"Call them and try and get a comment," he would say. "Just try."

I'd say a few choice words and—bam!—slam the phone down, make the call, and get a "Fort Hood officials declined to comment," which I knew was what I was going to get, and then Sig was satisfied.

We went our separate ways a long time ago, but Sig was one of the people I contacted when I was in one of my self-discovery modes and was asking select people what they thought of when they thought of me. I don't know myself, I said, so I'm asking people—how would you describe John Clark?

Sig offered a few flattering comments, mostly about my reporting and writing abilities, and he also said, "You know yourself better than you think you do. I think you need to live more and think less."

Pretty damn wise, if you ask me.

It's the end of week one in this positive thinking experiment. So far, I've implemented some but not all of the positive-habit-forming measures I decided on in the beginning. I have read a positive thinking message nearly every morning. I have managed to drink a tablespoon of olive oil and a tablespoon of lemon juice in the morning only two or three times. I have posted positive affirmation cards on my bathroom mirror. I have practice smiling. I have not done the mirror talk, nor have I volunteered my time somewhere—yet. I have played my guitar every day I was home this past week and even put on new strings today. Only went for one long walk, I guess, which was in Washington, D.C. I have been writing every day, except the time I was in Galveston. And I have not listened to positive thinking or deep sleep mediation CDs at bedtime, but I am starting tonight.

So I've made progress but have not achieved perfection. And that's OK. That's just fine.

Tomorrow and the rest of this week will be a challenge as I return to work and the pressure and stress that goes on there. I'm sure I'll relapse into some negative thinking and behaviors, but the key is to be aware of it as it happens and turn things around.

Progress, not perfection.

"Don't get upset with people or situations; both are powerless without your reaction."

Day Eight

Feeling good today. Went to bed early and was awake before the alarm went off at six. Read the affirmations on the bathroom mirror several times as I brushed my teeth and combed my hair.

"Live more; think less."

"Make the rest of your life the best of your life."

"Change your mind; change your life."

Powered up the laptop while I made coffee and drank my tablespoons of olive oil and lemon juice. Sat down and sipped a cup while checking book sales, email, and the latest news, then it was time to go. Off to a promising start.

Then I arrived at work.

I had been absent the day before last week's Thanksgiving holiday began, and my classroom was in a shambles. A dozen or so posters the youngsters have been working on for a novel we are reading were all over the floor. Desks and chairs were askew. It looked a bit like a tornado had blown through. Or a substitute teacher had been in charge.

Ah, yes, after a wonderful week of vacation and stress-relief, back to reality.

Time to straighten up.

It is roughly halfway through the day now, and I've done quite well maintaining my positive attitude—surprisingly well, in fact, despite being bombarded by a number of the usual frustrations and stress-inducers that normally send me over the edge, or at least close to it.

I'm not sure if it's because I am reminding myself to stay positive, and I'm not giving the negative thoughts time or room to grow and overwhelm. What's the old saying? No free rent inside my head? Or is it that I had a week of positive thinking practice to get ready for today?

Either way, I was in a good mood all day today, with only one brief and very minor meltdown from which I quickly recovered. One kid even looked at me at one point with a big smile on her face and said, "You're in a good mood, aren't you?"

After work, I did an interview for this Friday's newspaper column, then went home, changed clothes, and went outside and walked for 30 minutes. Didn't really want to but knew I needed to add one more thing to my list. I ate some leftovers and then spent most of the rest of the evening writing the column so I could get it out of the way. It's now 10:15 p.m., and I need to get my butt to bed or I might be old Mr. Grumpy tomorrow, which I don't want to be.

It was kind of nice today being in a good mood practically all day. Dare I say I enjoyed myself at work?

"The most important decision you make is to be in a good mood."

- Voltaire

Day Nine

> *"It all begins in your mind. What you think, you create."*

Today did not get off to a very positive start. In fact, to be honest, I was in a foul mood.

The day started with the alarm ringing at 4 a.m. because, when I went to bed, I pushed the wrong button. There are two alarm settings on my alarm clock, and the one I intended to set was for 6 a.m., but somehow I managed to push the other one.

So I rolled out of bed, feeling just fine, rested, alert, and ready to go. Went in and brushed my teeth, combed my hair, read the affirmations posted on the mirror a few times, and headed out to the kitchen to make coffee. When I got there, I saw the clock on the stove—4:10. I looked at it again, and then I looked over at the clock on the microwave. Same thing. What the hell? Then it dawned on me what must have happened.

Oh, you've got to be kidding.

I felt fine and could have—probably should have—stayed up and gotten some work done, but you know, four o'clock? And that bed is so comfortable.

Back to bed. Reset the alarm and off again to dreamland.

But that wasn't the reason for the foul mood. I was letting worry about something that had not happened yet have free rent in my head. And I know better.

Negative thoughts. Falling back into old habits. Old thinking patterns.

What is the old adage again—90 percent of what we worry about never even happens?

But, I chose not to let the negativity overwhelm me, concentrated on positive thoughts and energy, and things got better. And, of course, what I was worrying about and stressing over never happened at all. I really am learning…not how to control my thoughts, because I don't think we can control our thoughts, but how to react to negative thoughts in a positive way. Not dwell on them. Not let them grow and fester. Just acknowledge the thought, look at it, and let it go.

If needed, spray it with some positive thoughts. Negative thoughts dissolve in the spray of positive thoughts, I think.

I also got some wonderful news in the early afternoon—both the new books I submitted to my publisher for consideration were accepted and apparently are going to be published. At this time last year, I had one self-published book that had sold a total of maybe 30 copies. Right now, I have three books designed, published, and marketed by an actual publisher, with thousands of copies sold, and now it looks like two more on the way, with another two—including this one—in the works. A total of seven published books, and the dream of becoming a full-time author is moving closer and closer to reality.

I could never have imagined such a thing one year ago. Stuck in a job I hated, unable to see a way out of the quagmire. And now? The dream is on the horizon.

"Things you are passionate about are not random—they are calling you."

- Fabienne Fredrickson

Day Ten

"Instead of looking at what's depressing, look at what's a blessing."

Looking back and regretting.
Two common ways to feed negativity and stay miserable.

Oh, by the way, the thing I was worrying and stressing about yesterday? Well, it finally did happen, but it wasn't nearly as horrible as my monkey brain imagined it would. Surprise, surprise.

It was an annual evaluation at work, and it went great. One of the best evaluations in recent memory.

But I digress...

Looking back and regretting. I've always been a champion at both. I actually have the ability to go back in time and rehash situations from junior high and high school and kick myself for not doing things differently. Wondering what might have happened if I'd turned left instead of right, figuratively speaking.

I still wish I'd beat the hell out of a kid named Jimmy that day in the high school gym. I've replayed that scene over and over in my head. I know exactly what I should have done as he stood there with that smug look on his face, silently daring me to do something. We were about the same size, both skinny, but I was a much better athlete. I should have lowered my shoulder, rammed it into his midsection, wrapped my arms around him, lifted a little, and driven him all the way across the gym floor until he slammed backward into the wooden bleachers. Then, as he lay gasping for air on the polished floor, I should have pounded him with my fists. But I just stood there.

That jerk had some kind of mind control over me back then. I know for a fact life would have been different if that had happened. It's a pretty good fantasy, but it was 40 years ago, for heaven's sakes. And I'm still losing sleep over it? Good grief, man, get a grip.

Like my old friend Craig said, don't look back at the bad things. Only look back for the good. It's probably a good thing I didn't take Jimmy and slam him into the bleachers and then beat him senseless. Because I might have really hurt him. That's one reason I didn't get into any fights after 8th grade. I had a pretty violent temper.

One time in woodshop, a kid accidentally hacked me across the forearm with a little handheld saw. Scraped the skin but didn't draw blood. No big deal, really.

Well, I wheeled around with a small drill I was holding and slammed it into his leg. Luckily, the bit bounced off his kneecap, didn't penetrate his blue jeans or his leg. If the location of my stab had been a little different, I might have wound up in handcuffs, and who knows what kind of damage I could have done to that kid's leg.

So, it was a good day today at work, with the dreaded evaluation out of the way. It was also a bit of a letdown after all the anticipation and stress of not knowing, but again, that goes back to 90 percent of what we worry about never coming to pass. Worrying about things that are not even reality.

I still hope this is my last year as a teacher and that I will be able to afford to do nothing but write and publish books, put out a podcast, and maybe continue writing for the local paper. But now, if I have to continue in the classroom another year or two or more, I think it's going to be OK.

The public school system hasn't changed. In fact, it's more screwed up than ever. Parents are just as overinvolved, adversarial, demanding, and unreasonable as ever. Kids are still overprotected, coddled, and as entitled as ever. None of that has changed. The difference is my attitude. I think it's going to be OK.

Wait, check that. I *know* it's going to be OK.

"Forget what's gone, appreciate what still remains, and look forward to what's coming next."

Day Eleven

My way of thinking seems to be changing.

Today at school, as students in my last class of the day were listening to an audio recording of a novel, following along in their books, there was a part about a mother worried that her autistic teenage daughter would never learn the skills necessary to have a regular life.

I was at the head of the class, over to one side, sitting on a stool at my podium, and when I heard those words—for the umpteenth time—it suddenly occurred to me that I am truly grateful for my life. Even if it ended right now, it's been a great life—the good, the bad, and the ugly.

I've always been a bit of a disappointment to myself. I'm not afraid of dying, really, but I think afraid of dying with a load of regrets. I thought my life could have been so much different—so much better—if I hadn't been such an idiot when I was younger. If I'd made better decisions and not been so hardheaded, so rebellious, had such a bad attitude.

So afraid to be myself.

But guess what?

I've had a life, and a pretty damn good one at that, in spite of myself and because of myself. All my decisions weren't bad ones. I made some good moves. I've set goals and achieved them. I've loved and been loved. I've traveled and seen beautiful places. I've had three careers, all successful. I've never really failed at anything I set out to do.

I wanted to go to college, and I did—at age 26. I decided I wanted to study journalism and become a reporter. I earned my degree, and I was a newspaper reporter for fifteen years. Then, I decided I wanted something different, and after much contemplation, decided to become a schoolteacher. That took a bit of a leap of faith because I had to quit my job in order to complete the final course requirements to be able to get my teaching certificate. But I did it, and now I'm in my thirteenth year in education.

Now I have my sights set on my fourth career—author. And that is a big part of the reason for this positive thinking campaign. It would be really easy for me to talk myself out of believing that this dream could come true. Me? A full-time author? No going to work somewhere every day? No boss to worry about? Sure, other people do it, but me? You've got to be kidding.

But if I believe it will happen, it will happen. I am pretty sure of that. I just have to believe and put in the work.

> *"Positive thinking makes a broken life beautiful."*

Day Twelve

Tried a little meditation today at lunch. Nothing major. About ten minutes' worth. But I liked it. I always have, the times I've tried it. I just never stuck with it long enough to do any good.

I remember interviewing a holistic guy in Odessa, Texas, when I was doing research for my first book, and he told me it takes about two weeks of consistent meditation to begin to notice the effects. I'm going to do it. I know how—it's just a matter of doing it.

Not a whole lot to report today, honestly. It's been a long week—a good week, but a long one—and I'm looking forward to a good long sleep tonight. That's about it.

So today I'll keep it short and leave you with a quote from Winston Churchill, the famous prime minister of England from 1940-45 and 1951-55:

"Success is not final; failure is not fatal. It is the courage to continue that counts."

Day Thirteen

Saturday.

A day for relaxation.

Completed a couple of chores—laundry and grocery shopping. Then it was time to write and watch some football. Dozed off a little bit during the football watching, which was good. The napping was good, not so much the football. I got a little bored watching Alabama win yet another game and their opponent not make it very difficult for them to do so. So, I went in and took a nice, warm bath (I love baths), and then did a little meditation.

Again, only about ten minutes, but it felt really good. I got into a very relaxed state and felt myself smiling as I listened to a woman with a soft voice recite instructions and affirmations. I might even have been a little hypnotized, as it was difficult to open my eyes when she counted one, two, three.

Basic meditation is easy and centers around concentrating on the breath. You can sit in any number of positions: on the floor with your legs crossed or folded under you, like you see in pictures; on the floor with legs out straight and back resting against a chair or couch; in a chair, feet flat on the floor, hands resting wherever it is most comfortable.

I sat in a sturdy chair, feet flat on the ground, hands in my lap. After a while, I felt the urge to let my hands fall down to my sides. After a minute or two, they wanted to return to my lap, so I put them there again.

Close your eyes and simply breathe in and out, focusing your mind on the breathing. In and out. However you want to do it. In through the nose and out through the mouth; in through the mouth and out through the nose; in and out through the nose; in and out through the mouth. It really doesn't matter, in my opinion. Choose whatever works best for you. Whatever is most comfortable. But focus your mind completely on your breathing.

Focus on the air going in and coming out. Focus on your chest rising and falling with each breath. Feel the air enter and exit your body. Focus on it.

Try not to think of anything else. Just your breath.

If you're like me, thoughts will invade—they always do. Today, of course, I was thinking of a couple of things that happened yesterday. I am so good at reliving the past! The trick is to acknowledge the thought, take a look at it, and let it disappear. Just let that pesky thought slide right on through. Don't focus on it, and it will leave. Just keep focusing on the breath.

It also is a great idea to repeat an affirmation as you sit with your eyes closed, breathing normally, focusing on your breath. There are thousands of affirmations, and I've listed thirteen good ones here. Why thirteen? Because that's my lucky number. I think because I was born on the thirteenth.

The "I Am" affirmations are said to be powerful and influential for the subconscious mind. Pick one of these or make up one of your own. Recite it over and over in your mind as you breathe and feel the air enter and exit. Set a timer of some sort for however long you want to meditate. Maybe start with ten minutes and increase that by a couple of minutes when you think you're ready.

Try it for two weeks, every day. See if you notice any results. Feeling less stressed? Calmer, more relaxed? More confident?

This is only Day Two for me, so I'll let you know in ten more days. Here are some affirmations:

I am grateful for my life.

I am happy and successful.

I am worthy of being loved.

I am safe.

I am at peace with the universe and with myself.

I am strong.

I am attractive.

I am talented.

I am confident.

I am beautiful.

I am blessed with wonderful family and friends.

I am conquering my illness.

I am at peace with my past and excited about my future.

Good luck. May peace and a positive mind be with you.

"Change your mind; change your life."

Day Fourteen

I almost swapped out today's opening affirmation for a different one after finishing my ten minutes of meditation just now. But I think this is a good one, because I've spent most of the weekend writing. I've been working on this book, and a couple of hours ago I finished my column for next Friday's paper. Later this evening, I will do some more work on *Destination Unknown*, the book on what people think about death and dying.

That's been pretty much my whole weekend—aside from washing clothes, buying some groceries, ironing four shirts, playing my guitar for a little while (still trying to build up the calluses on my left hand), watching a little football, and thawing out some fish for dinner.

And part of me says, "You spent your whole weekend doing that?"

Is it worth it?

The answer is, yes—for two reasons.

First: writers write. If you are truly a writer, you write, no matter what, because writing is not a means to an end. It is the process of writing, expressing yourself, feeding the soul that matters. That is the important part. Not the outcome.

Second: even though, in some ways, becoming a full-time, self-supporting author with no day job needed seems far-fetched, part of me is starting to believe it's going to happen. Other people's dreams come true—why not mine? Two things will make it a reality, both of which come from me: believing it is possible and putting in the work.

That is one reason I embarked on this positive thinking campaign in the first place. My monkey brain can really get carried away with itself, and I have to believe with all my heart that I can do it. There is no room for negativity. I'm starting to get there. Making progress.

Hence, today's opening affirmation. I haven't told many people about my dream because too many people are negative about dreams. Too many people stop believing in dreams. I work with someone who apparently has no dreams. I asked her last Friday what she was going to do over the weekend. She said she was going to sleep. All weekend? That's it?

"I don't have anything else to do," she said, shrugging her shoulders.

My friend, Bobby, never gave up on his dream, even after nearly losing it all a time or two over the years. He believed in himself and stayed positive. His dream finally came true. It took 30 years of hard work, but it came true.

Life is all about the journey, folks, not the destination. It's all about the journey.

What is your dream?

"A negative mind will never give you a positive life."

Day Fifteen

Sort of a restless night's sleep, and when the alarm went off this morning before I wanted it to, I had to resist my natural impulse to let out a groan and say something like, "Crap, I don't feel like getting up. I don't want to go to work."

I am convinced now that starting off the day with such a comment pretty much guarantees a bad day. Or at least significantly increases the chances. So what did I do? I wanted to hit the snooze button and delay the inevitable. Just for a few more minutes...

The negative thoughts came into my head, no denying that. They were absolutely there. But, unlike the past, I didn't have to give those thoughts any room. They came into my head, and I looked at them, acknowledged them, and I said, "No, I'm not going to give you a voice. I'm not going to give you any power."

No power over me. No power over my attitude. No power over my day. So what did I do?

Instead, I said, "It's going to be a great day." Said it out loud, even though I wasn't entirely convinced, then I rolled over, put my feet on the floor, and started my morning routine.

Positive thoughts = positive results.

And, sure enough, it turned out to be a pretty damn good day.

Not much else to report, really. Just a little verification that positive thinking produces positive results. It was a routine day, but a good day.

It's all in the attitude. Like my hero, John Lennon, said in his wonderful song, "Beautiful Boy":

"Life is what happens to you when you're busy making other plans."

Life is life. It's not so much what happens to you, it's how you deal with what happens to you that is important.

Positive thinking, y'all. Positive thoughts. Always positive.

New way of thinking. New habits.

"The greatest weapon against unhappiness is our ability to choose one thought over another."

Day Sixteen

What if today were your last day on Earth?

What would you do?

How would you spend the time?

We've all heard that before. But it's a really good question. And wouldn't it be nice to truly live one day at a time. Just enjoying each moment, each little thing, with no concerns about what happened yesterday and no worries about tomorrow.

Some people are able to do that, I suppose. I sure can't.

This old guy I used to know would say, "If you've got one foot in yesterday and one foot in tomorrow, you're gonna piss all over today."

I've pissed all over plenty of todays.

If I knew that today was my last day on Earth and tomorrow I'd be dead…that's a tough one. Having at least a week's notice would be nice.

I think I'd want to wind up on the beach, at the ocean. That's where I'd like to die. Before that, though, I'd like to see some friends, give them a hug, and tell them I love them. I'd want to spend time with my daughters and my stepsons. They're spread out all over the world, so that's why I'd like a little more advance notice.

My wife, that goes without saying. She'd be there with me on the beach, holding my hand as I watched the waves and went wherever we go when we die.

I'm writing a book about that very subject right now—what happens when we die. I'm interviewing people from all over the country and the world, as many places as I can manage, about what they believe happens. I think it's going to be an excellent book.

Since most of us will never know exactly when our time is to run out, all we can do, I think, is to try to make the most of each day as it comes. Working at a job you love is a heckuva good start, since most of us have to work to live. Such has not been the case for me in recent years, and so I've been working hard to change my attitude, and I've made a lot of progress in the past few months. I don't love my job now, but I really don't hate it anymore. Hating your job and dreading going to work is a miserable way to live.

One big way to live a happy life is to set a goal that makes your life worthwhile, something that gives it meaning, and work toward achieving it. Something that makes it worthwhile and meaningful to you, not to someone else. Do something every day that moves you closer to achieving that goal. It may take a long time to get there, but there is satisfaction in the doing.

There is a famous quote by a guy named Joseph M. Dodge:

"What every man needs, regardless of his job or the kind of work he is doing, is a vision of what his place is and may be. He needs an objective and a purpose. He needs a feeling and a belief that he has some worthwhile thing to do. What this is, no one can tell him. It must be his own creation."

I read somewhere a long time ago a piece of advice about how to live one's life with the fewest regrets. Some old dude said that whenever you come to a fork in the road, a place where a decision needs to be made, you should imagine yourself old and dying, on your deathbed, looking back at your life and the choices you made. Then make your decision based on what your old and dying self would tell you to do.

> *"Every day, do something that moves you closer to your dreams."*

Day Seventeen

"Don't worry about finding happiness...just be happy and it will find you."

Woke up feeling good today for no apparent reason. I just kind of felt good inside. Happy. Used to be one of those things that gave me pause for concern, maybe even confused me a little bit. I'm not used to feeling good inside for no reason. It's a strange sensation, but I'm getting used to it.

So it's a little after six o'clock in the morning, and I'm sitting here with some coffee—need to start getting ready for work in a few minutes—and I get a Facebook message from my South African friend, Nix, who is currently on an island somewhere in the Caribbean. I met this free-spirited young woman in Spain during my first walk on the Camino de Santiago pilgrimage.

Crossing paths with her was among the life-changing experiences I wrote about in my book, *Camino: Laughter and Tears Along Spain's Camino de Santiago Pilgrimage*. It was a few days after we happened to spend the night at the same albergue, and Nix was among five of us who had dinner together. We went our separate ways from there, until one afternoon my friend Tom and I walked into the beautiful backyard of another albergue, 50 miles or so down the road, and there was Nix, clothespins in her mouth, hanging up freshly washed laundry.

I never thought I'd see her again, and so it was a pleasant surprise. My feet were killing me that day, and I had a few pretty nice blisters, and I asked Nix if she had a needle and thread I could use to treat them. You thread the needle, then run it through the blister and leave some thread running through so it doesn't close back up, and then it dries out and goes away. No more blister.

Nix said, sure, no problem, and went back inside the albergue to fetch the needle and thread, and when she came back out, she asked if I wanted her to do it. OK, I said, and propped my foot up in a white plastic lawn chair. Nix stood there and carefully tended my aching feet. I thanked her and she said no problem and that was that.

But the more I thought about it, the more moved I was by her gesture. I hardly knew this girl from halfway around the world, and here she was, in the middle of nowhere in Spain, gently and carefully doctoring my blisters. It was almost biblical.

Nix was no longer outside, so I went in and found her sitting at one of the coin-operated computers up front, checking her e-mail or something, and I put my hands on her shoulders, said thank you again, and kissed her on top of the head.

We've stayed in touch ever since, and she messaged me just now about doing a Skype interview for my new book, *Destination Unknown*. She will be a great interview, and I also have a guy from Louisiana lined up who apparently is a medium who communicates all the time with the dead. Another great story!

The biggest problem I'm having right now is time. There just isn't enough time in the day to do everything I need to do. When I started this experiment, I created a list of ten things to do each day to help foster a more positive attitude. Of those ten, I probably get half done every day.

I always read a positive message in the morning, and I drink my olive oil and lemon juice mixture for good health. I have posted my affirmation cards on the bathroom mirror, and I read those every morning. I have practiced smiling a few times, but not every day—certainly not enough to form a habit of smiling. I have not done the mirror talk (probably resisting this one subconsciously). Have not volunteered my time yet. Have played my guitar, but not every day. Have not been going for long walks every day but have been listening to positive thinking or deep sleep meditation CDs at bedtime.

And I truly think it's working. Negative thought patterns are still there, but it's like they're off in the distance, in the back of my head somewhere, sort of in the shadows. I can easily ignore them. Maybe my head is full of positive thoughts, and they're edging out the negativity, I don't know. I do know one thing.

I like it.

"No matter how long we have traveled on the wrong road, we can always turn around."

Day Eighteen

> *"Good things are coming. Just keep going."*

G otta be honest. Not really feeling it today. Not feeling real positive and good like I have been. So it's a really good time for today's lead-off affirmation.

One day at a time. One foot in front of the other. Do the right thing and keep moving. Everything else will take care of itself.

Nothing in particular has gone wrong. Didn't get a very good night's sleep is about the only thing I can think of that went wrong. Nothing I can put my finger on, really. Just one of those days. And here's the deal:

This, too, shall pass.

Tomorrow's another day. Another chance.

I have several interviews scheduled over the weekend for *Destination Unknown*. Work is going well. My wife is coming home Monday after being on the road for two months. And she apparently has a new job secured that will not require traveling, which is very good. I do OK around here by myself, but it gets lonely.

The holidays are upon us. Christmas is two weeks away, and that means road trips down to Houston and Galveston to see Bobby and Joe and Craig. I'm sure my youngest daughter will come hang out for a while, although my oldest will be in North Carolina. All in all, who could ask for more? Good friends, family, two weeks' vacation…

Blessings all around.

Count your blessings, y'all, count your blessings. There are lots of them.

> *"Surround yourself with people who make you happy."*

Day Nineteen

"*Growth can be painful. Change can be painful. But nothing is as painful as staying stuck.*"

This affirmation seems especially appropriate today.

I guess I'm in a little slump or something. I think I know what the common denominator is, and it's completely fixable, so no worries there. The only thing to do is just keep on keepin' on.

This, too, shall pass.

One thing that could be coming into play, darkening my skies, so to speak, is the holiday season. Work always gets more stressful this time of year, and I have a bit of a hard time in general with the holidays. A lot of it is probably my fault. There are things I can do to make it better.

When I was a kid, Christmas was magical, of course. Even after I found out Santa wasn't real, it was still a helluva lot of fun. Lots of presents under the tree. Lights and decorations everywhere. Mama cooking a big meal: turkey, stuffing, mashed potatoes, gravy, cranberry sauce, candied yams, black olives, green olives, little sweet pickles, stuffed celery, cherry pie, pumpkin pie, all that good stuff. House full of people.

Even when my brother, sister, and I got older and moved out on our own, and our parents got divorced, Mama's was the place to go for the holidays. Now that she's gone, things are just not the same.

But, really, without Mama around to liven up the holidays, it's up to me to carry on and start new traditions. It can never be anywhere close to the same—especially since I no longer have a relationship with my sister or my brother and haven't seen or talked to either one of them in years, and my kids and my wife's kids are spread out all over the country and overseas—but if I put a little more effort into it, I imagine I'd be a little more holly jolly.

I said I was going to put up some Christmas lights on the house this year but still haven't done it. Pull some of the decorations down from the attic and make things a little festive. We haven't done any of that in a long time.

So, I'm more than halfway through this positive thinking project, and I can honestly say that things have improved. No question about it. Yesterday and today are not very good indicators, but like I said, just a bit of a slump, not a downhill plunge. Maybe the barometric pressure in the atmosphere is low, or something is disrupting my biorhythms or something. We haven't had much sunshine in a while. Who knows?

Just keep doing the right thing. Keep moving forward.

This, too, shall pass.

"Everything comes to you at the right time. Be patient and trust in the process."

Day Twenty

Today was a great day.

The past two days were not so good, but remember—this too, shall, pass. And so it did.

Slept in this morning with no alarm to jar me from sleep, which is always a good thing. After coffee, eggs, and biscuits, I headed out into the country to check out a bunch of kids learning to target shoot in a 4H shooting club. It was a dreary, damp, overcast morning, but the little ranch I went to about 30 minutes from where I live was beautiful, in a rock-strewn, cactus-filled, horseshit-littered kind of way.

I was there taking pictures for a photo essay for next week's paper, and I was supposed to stick around after to interview one of the instructors about his horse-training business for a feature story for next week. After about two hours, the target practice was still going on, so I bugged out and told the guy we could try again next week for the horse-training story.

Came back home, dozed on and off on the couch for a few hours, and then called a guy in Shreveport, Louisiana, to do an interview for my book, *Destination Unknown: What Happens After You Die?*

I've never met this guy, who is the brother of an old high school classmate. Suzanne sat in front of me in English class and, oh my goodness, she was fine. After talking with her brother today for about 45 minutes, I found out why she was so beautiful. The family heritage is Native American and Creole. Give me a minute. I'm reminiscing a bit…

OK, back to business.

This guy, my old classmate's brother, is a psychic medium. I chat with Suzanne once in a while on Facebook and asked her recently if she'd let me interview her for the book. She said, "Sure, but you really should talk to my brother."

I am so glad I asked her.

It was an amazing conversation. Lifted my mood just talking to him. He has been communicating with spirits since he was a kid, and now he does psychic readings for people interested in talking with family members and friends who are no longer here. I purposely don't say dead family members and friends because I tend to believe that life goes on somehow after people leave planet Earth. So does he.

This psychic medium says he stops short of saying that there is life after death, but he knows for a fact that the soul continues on with all the memories of life experiences here on Earth. He knows this because they speak to him, they talk to the people they leave behind, the living, and he relays their messages.

For some, this is a far-fetched concept, and a lot of people would say this guy is crazy, and even that such things are demonic. I say that is a closed-minded attitude. Who really knows what happens after we die?

He is a lifelong Catholic and still believes in the religion of his youth. He believes in heaven and hell, God and Jesus, all of that. And he also believes that for some reason, he was blessed with the gift of being a channel for those who have gone to the other side. For some reason, they speak to him, and he can hear them.

I believe him because I believe that anything is possible.

Even me changing from a pessimist to an optimist.

"It takes only one person to change your life. You."

Day Twenty-One

> *"Life only comes around once, so do whatever makes you happy,
> and be around those who make you smile."*

We were having eggs and toast and grits and coffee and orange juice one Saturday morning at the Star Drug Store in downtown Galveston, the oldest drug store in Texas. It was me, Joe, and Bobby on one of our boys' weekends, and we were talking about making positive changes and learning to be happy.

All of a sudden, Bobby puts his hands out on the table, about two feet apart and says, "Look, imagine this is a timeline." Oh, brother, I knew exactly what was coming next.

"I don't want to do the timeline thing," I said. He continued, anyway.

"Let's say this timeline is 88 years long," he said. "Let's say that's how long you, Joe, and I are going to live …"

"Hey, there are 88 keys on a piano!" Joe, a talented keyboard player, chimes in.

Bobby looks at him, grins, and shakes his head.

"So this is 88 years," he says, then moving his hands closer together, removing about two-thirds of the timeline. "Here's how much you've got left. How much longer you gonna wait?"

I'd known that was coming, but even so, it made an impression because he was right.

How much longer you gonna wait to be happy? When it comes down to it, it's all about making a decision. Be happy. Just do it.

I'm working hard to be happy and make positive changes, and this book is part of the effort. I'm not all the way there yet, but I'm making progress. And that's what counts.

We seek progress, not perfection.

Ten days left in the experiment, including the rest of today, and it's time to make a final, concentrated push to the finish line. Sort of like that distance runner rounding the final turn. Time to make that kick and push hard to the tape. I haven't done each and every one of my initial ten positive thinking exercises on a daily basis, but I've put a good dent in the list.

I read a positive message every morning. I drink my olive oil and lemon juice. I've posted affirmation cards. I've practiced smiling. These next ten days, I will do the mirror talk every day. I have yet to volunteer my time somewhere—there are only so many hours in the day, after all. I have played my guitar, but not every day. I have not gone for very many long walks. I have listened to positive thinking of deep sleep meditation CDs at bedtime, but not every night.

Progress, not perfection.

Before this all started, I was doing none of those things. Not on a daily basis, an every-other-day basis, or any basis. And it's working. It's working.

"Whatever your past, let go of it, and start a new, better beginning. You are open and ready to receive all that is good."

Day Twenty-Two

*"You can't calm the storm. So stop trying.
What you can do is calm yourself. The storm will pass."*

I've always been one to let the storm kick my ass. To get all worked up about things that are not going right, or the way I want them to go, and just whipping myself into a frenzy.

When my youngest daughter was born, the doctor said, "Uh-oh," as he was examining her (you never want to hear a doctor or a dentist say, "uh-oh"), and they soon found a problem with her eyes. She was perfect in every way, but there was a cloudiness covering one of her eyes.

It was not good, but nothing could be determined for sure until she was seen by an eye specialist the next day. Me? I freaked out, of course. Immediately thought the worst. "What if she's blind?" I wailed. "What are we gonna do?"

My mother was there. She put her hand on my shoulder and said softly, "Don't borrow trouble, son."

Don't borrow trouble.

Indeed, everything turned out to be OK, although the baby did require some ongoing treatments. She is healthy and happy and normal and not blind today. But I kept borrowing trouble for the next few decades.

When I get home this evening, I may or may not complete the tasks I was planning—long walk, meditation, playing my guitar—because my wife is coming home today after being away on business for two months. We were together for a few days over Thanksgiving, but I imagine there still is going to be some making-up-for-lost-time to do.

But things are going well. Three more days until two weeks' Christmas vacation.

It doesn't get any better than that.

"The difference between a good day and a bad day is your attitude."

Day Twenty-Three

> *"A river cuts through rock not because of its power, but because of its persistence.*
> *You can achieve anything you want as long as you keep trying."*

G otta be honest—today's not one of those real positive days. I'm a little tired, a little cranky. Didn't sleep well at all last night. I don't want to embarrass my wife but last night was the first time she's been home in two months, and she snores like a damn freight train. Normally, I use these little silicone ear plugs to try to drown out the roaring sound, but apparently I don't have any more. I looked all over.

I finally had to go sleep in another room, and that wasn't a whole lot better.

It's not all her fault, though. I have trouble sleeping under the best conditions. A classic example of how light a sleeper I am is the time something woke me up in the middle of the night, and I realized that what had woken me from a perfectly good sleep was the sound of our dog out on the back porch, crunching on dog food.

I'm not kidding.

But I digress…

Today also includes a heavy dose of sadness mixed with gratitude.

I found out yesterday that someone close to me—a young man, unrelated, but someone I have known since he was a little kid—is facing a prison sentence after attempting to drive home drunk from a bar and killing a father of two with his pickup. The news was devastating, incredibly sad, and heartbreaking. He apparently doesn't even remember the crash.

One thing that definitely came to mind was the old adage, "There but for the grace of God go I."

That could have been me any number of times. Many times.

Why him? How did I manage to get away with the same thing for years? Why was I spared the same fate? Was someone watching over me?

I don't know, but life goes on today. The sun is shining. Some people are at work; others are getting ready for the holidays. Cleaning, shopping, cooking, wrapping, decorating, whatever. But that young man is sitting in a jail cell, and his life and the life of that family are changed forever. Maybe not ruined completely, but changed forever.

I'm so incredibly sad, and also truly grateful that never happened to me.

"When there's no turning back, we should concern ourselves only with the best way of going forward."

Day Twenty-Four

> *"Maybe the journey isn't so much about becoming anything. Maybe it's about unbecoming everything that isn't really you, so you can be who you were meant to be in the first place."*

Another truth that fits me like a glove...

Hey, I just remembered, it's been ten days since I started the meditations with the "I Am" affirmations, and I said I'd report back. To be honest, I haven't noticed any startling results yet. Nothing dramatic or earth shattering. Undoing a lifetime of negative thinking takes a while, I suspect.

The secret is to just keep going.

I do feel a little better, though.

I'm thinking I might even hang in there a little while longer with the teaching thing. The money's not bad. The vacation time is great. And the longer I stay, the better my pension gets. I don't know. We'll see what happens over the next six months.

Meanwhile, it's about time right now for a warm bubble bath and then some couch time. I had a crumbling tooth hacked out of my head a couple hours ago, and had to drive back to the dentist after my mouth wouldn't stop filling up with blood. It looks like somebody emptied a small can of red paint in the flower bed next to my front porch. They got things straightened out, but the numbness is starting to wear off, and I imagine it's going to start hurting. I took a couple of nice pain pills, but lying down for a while couldn't hurt.

All in all, it's been a great day. I almost said a good day, but really it's been a great day. I'm blessed to be healthy, no issues other than being a little overweight and having ongoing dental excitement due to my own neglect during my younger days. I'm safe, living in a nice, quiet neighborhood where if you forget and leave the front door unlocked or the garage door open, nothing unusual happens.

I'm warm and dry, even though it's drizzly and 30-something degrees outside. I can see. I can hear. I can talk. My sense of smell is not very good, but a lot of times, that's not a bad thing at all. I know how to read and write in two languages. I have a nice, comfortable bed, although that mattress could probably be replaced—and I have the money to do that, if I ever decide to do so. I have a nice vehicle to drive. A good job. Money in the bank. I have food and water, electricity. When I go to the grocery store, I can basically buy whatever I want. I have a closet full of clothes.

I have a woman who loves me. My two daughters are healthy and happy, and they love me and actually think I am a good dad. I have two stepsons who respect me and consider me a father.

I have the freedom to go and do whatever I want. If I want to drive to Louisiana this weekend and eat Cajun food and gamble at the casino, I can do that. If I want to fly to Las Vegas for a couple of days, I can do that. Take a road trip over to Colorado and look at the mountains? No problem. Next summer, I am taking my third trip to Europe—my third trip! I never seriously imagined I would ever go to Europe even one time.

I'm really blessed, and if you stop and think about it, I'll bet you are, too.

"A moment of gratitude makes a difference in your attitude."

Day Twenty-Five

> *"The key to happiness is letting each situation be what it is instead of what you think it should be.*
>
> - Mandy Hale

For a long time, I lived in a sort of unreality. If things were not as I wanted them to be, I was pissed and wondered why. "The world sucks," I said.

If people didn't behave a certain way or meet my expectations, I rejected them. Crossed them off the list. In my baseball game of life, it was one strike and you're out. "People suck," I said.

Especially in relationships with other people, I never learned the art of negotiation or compromise. When I was a kid, I didn't have to compromise. I didn't have to try to make friends. They were just there. I was a popular kid, a star athlete. I hung out with the other little studs, and people wanted to hang out with us, be our friends. We could pick and choose. If you don't like it, move out of the way or get run over.

As I got older, of course, and my world got a little bigger, there were people who didn't like me. No reason for it, necessarily. Sometimes, people just don't like other people. That's the way the world works. I didn't understand that. I always thought everyone should like me. If someone didn't, it bothered me—a lot.

Kind of the same thing with situations. I had a tendency to see things the way I wanted them to be instead of the way they actually were. I lived for two-and-a-half years with a master manipulator and sociopath, who literally turned me every which way but loose.

After some friends sort of intervened and helped me get out of there, I still went back for more. I wanted her back. She took full advantage of this, of course, and continued to squeeze me for everything she could get. I met a wonderful woman who loved me and wanted to take care of me, and I still wanted the psycho.

I was talking to a friend about it one day, and he looked at me with kind of an amused expression and said, "Let me get this straight. You've got this one girl who treats you like a king, and you've got this other one who treats you like dirt. Where's the decision, man?"

I eventually dragged myself out of that quagmire, met another woman on a blind date, and we've been married now for fourteen years. Not always happily married, mostly because we both brought too much baggage on the trip, but definitely happily married today. I still have a little trouble sometimes with the reality thing—seeing things for what they are, instead of what I want them to be, or wish they were. But I'm getting better at it.

And isn't that what it's all about? Getting better all the time.

"If you're trying your best, you're doing just fine."

Day Twenty-Six

Another big key for me. Never being happy with myself, what I have, or what I've accomplished. Always comparing myself to other people and basing my opinion of myself on what others think about me.

Back when I was young and dumb and working as an engineering draftsman, one of the first questions I'd ask when I met someone new was what they did for a living. Then, I'd put them in a category. That was one of the ways I sorted people out. My own private caste system or something.

I knew where they ranked, and I knew where I ranked.

Of course, I almost always ranked myself in the top tier because I had a good job that paid well. People were impressed when they found out where I worked and what I did. That was important. What they thought of me was extremely important.

Unfortunately, I'm still that way to a certain extent. I still want people to like me. People that don't really matter. People who couldn't care less what I think about them, and in reality, probably don't think that much about me at all. People at work, for example. Most of them are just that, people at work. A few are friends who genuinely care about me, and I care about them. Those are the ones who matter. But part of me still wants that old approval from everyone. Part of me still seeks acknowledgment of my value from what others think.

I admire people who seem to genuinely not care what others think about them. Some people take it too far, but it must be nice to not let the opinion of others affect you one way or the other. To be that confident and self-assured.

But I'll keep working on it. We seek progress not perfection.

> *"Maybe people point out what's wrong with you because they can't handle all that's right with you."*

Day Twenty-Seven

Many moons ago, I was stewing over making a decision about something I can't even remember anymore, when a guy told me, "Listen to your gut. Just listen to what your gut tells you. Your gut never lies."

He was right, and I've followed—and given out—that simple and golden advice ever since.

Intuition is what it really is, and we all have it. That little voice inside that tries to guide and help us.

The psychic I interviewed a week ago for *Destination Unknown* talked about guardian angels. I believe in that. I believe that could be the source of the little voice inside that tries to steer us in the right direction. Apparently, there also are guardian devils or something because I don't know about you, but I sometimes have a little voice that tries to steer me in the wrong direction, as well.

Generally, though, even if you have both, the guardian angel speaks just a little louder, and that's why in our hearts, we usually know right from wrong.

If it feels wrong, it's probably wrong. If it feels right, go with it.

- Listen to your gut. Your gut never lies.

If you don't trust your gut, get a second opinion. Talk to someone about your decision. Sometimes, just talking about a problem or situation out loud makes the answer seem obvious.

- Write down the pros and cons.

Make a list. Two columns. Good and bad results of your proposed decision. If I do this, then this will happen. If I do that, then here's what will happen. Writing things down can help a lot.

- Sleep on it. Things will look different in the morning.

Great advice when faced with a decision. Talk it over with someone, and wait until tomorrow to decide.

When it comes down to it, you'll know deep down inside which way to go. Think about all the times you've ignored your gut when making a decision. When it just didn't feel right, but you went ahead and did it anyway. Probably didn't work out so well.

And, if you make the wrong move, it's never the end of the world. Everyone makes mistakes. The trick is to learn from those mistakes. That's what life is all about.

If you are doing your best, you're doing OK.

"It's OK. Some of the best days of your life haven't happened yet. Just keep going."

Day Twenty-Eight

> *"If you have family who loves you, a few good friends, and a roof over your head, you are richer than you think."*

I am way richer than I think.

Family who loves me. Check. A few good friends. Check. A roof over my head. Check.

The list goes on, but we did the gratitude thing back on Thanksgiving Day, remember? Have you made your gratitude list? There's a section at the end of this book to help with that.

Really, it's not a one-time thing, gratitude. I'm convinced that if you can practice an attitude of gratitude long enough and consistently enough for it to become a habit, you can't help but be a more positive person. Especially starting the day with thoughts of gratitude. Even one thankful thought.

Here's an idea. I haven't tried this one yet because I honestly just now thought of it.

Upon awakening in the morning, along with saying, "Today is going to be a great day," also say something for which you are grateful. Just one thing from your list. Maybe two. Like this:

"Today is a great day. I'm healthy, and I have a job."

When I started saying, "Today is going to be a great day," I said it several times, and I really didn't mean it. But after a while, it starts to work. The subconscious starts to believe it, and so it becomes fact. It becomes true. What is that old saying?

Life is not so much what happens to you, but how you react to the things that happen to you.

There are people in this world in what would seem to be miserable circumstances who are happy. Really happy. They are happy because they choose to be happy. It's a decision. The best decision you can make today is deciding to be happy.

I've got a helluva head cold today, and one side of my mouth is still hurting from Wednesday's oral surgery adventure, so I'm probably going to do quite a bit of couch time today, watching some NFL football, and not much else. It's a little cold outside, and my heater is pumping warm air into the house. I just finished a nice cup of coffee with some of that sweet creamer. The wife kissed me three times before she left for church a few minutes ago (I'm not a church guy). Both my daughters called me yesterday.

There is food in the fridge and in the pantry. I'll have a nice bowl of oatmeal here in a little while, after I make a phone call about my other book. Speaking of books, I should have three new ones out there sometime next month. I have a little money in my pocket and a little in the bank.

Today is Sunday, and I still have two weeks' vacation before I go back to work. Paid vacation.

I'm way richer than I think.

And, I suspect, so are you.

> "One small positive thought in the morning can change your whole day."

Day Twenty-Nine

Back to my friend, Bobby, one more time.

It was a year or two ago, over breakfast down in Galveston again—different place, this one a little hole-in-the-wall joint on 61st Street—when Bobby, Joe, and I were talking about me writing a newspaper column about our friendship. Three middle-aged guys who have known each other since we were kids, still keeping in touch and hanging out.

All weekend, as we played golf, ate fresh seafood, walked barefoot in the shallow surf, and rode across the bay in his new ski boat, Bobby had been saying, "This doesn't suck, does it?" That became our theme for the weekend, and I ended my column that week with his explanation of what it means:

"To me, 'it doesn't suck' means you've got to look for the non-sucky things," he said. "Some people only see the negative things in life. Here at Galveston, people always talk about the seaweed. Sure, the seaweed comes in and piles up on the beach, and it smells bad, but that's only for three months of the year. Unfortunately, it's the three months—June, July, and August—when a lot of people come here. The rest of the year, the beach is gorgeous, and I have pictures to prove it.

"What about the sun setting over the bay? Seagulls and pelicans flying overhead? The smell of the salt water. All the cool little shops and restaurants. Drive down to the west end and look at all the beautiful houses. The amazing history of Galveston. Dolphins swimming in the harbor; cruise ships sailing in and out.

"There's a lot more positive than negative—and that's just like life. You go through life looking for shit, and you'll find it."

It's all about attitude. Amazing that I'm finally learning that so late in life. Late in life, maybe, but not too late. Never too late.

I'm even getting to the point where I might be able to honestly say that I wouldn't change a thing. Wouldn't change a thing about my life, because every stupid thing I did, every boneheaded decision I made, every dumb move I made, led me to where I am now and to be the person I am today. And today, I'm a pretty good person.

Some people figure things out early—or seem to—and live what seem to be charmed lives. For others, like me, it takes a little longer.

In life, I think, it's not so much the destination, but the journey that counts. Hell, we all end up in the same place, when you come right down to it. But even though I've had lots of ups and downs, put myself through years of pain and suffering, hurt other people and myself, like my buddy Craig says, I was learning.

I still have unfulfilled goals and dreams, and there are a lot more birthdays behind me than in front of me, but that's OK. It is having those goals and dreams and working toward their fulfillment that counts. If I get there someday, what a celebration it will be. In the meantime, I'm going to happily pursue them and continue learning to be the best person I can be.

It's never too late.

"Life is too short to worry about stupid things. Have fun. Regret nothing. Don't rush. Never settle. If it's meant to be, it will be."

Day Thirty

Fear of failure is something I always scoffed at, but I think it is something I suffered from for a long time. And maybe still do, in some ways.

When I was fourteen years old, I was to be starting quarterback for a very good teenage football team at the Oaks Dads' Club in Houston. This team was legendary around town and used to beat the snot out of everybody. Never lost a game, ever.

I was backup quarterback when I was thirteen, and the next year I was the incumbent starter. And I lacked confidence. I was intimidated. One night at practice, I was struggling and the coach was on my ass. This guy was old school and didn't mind humiliating his players in front of God and the world. One time, this big, clumsy kid started puking as the team huddled up around the coach during a break in practice.

Our practices were brutal, and he had warned us not to eat before practice, but wait until after. When this kid starting puking all over his shoes, the coach was merciless.

"There you go, Lloyd, there you go! You sick, Lloyd? Well, there's your damn supper!"

Merciless.

If he had just ripped into me that night in front of the team and all the watching parents—some of whom didn't try very hard to conceal their amusement—it might not have been so bad. But when he walked past me and grumbled rather loudly, "We're gonna have to get a new quarterback," that was it.

I wound up quitting the team the next day, despite massive protestations from my dad. He didn't want me to quit for a number of reasons, one of which was his belief that once someone learns to quit, it becomes easier and easier to quit the next time.

And he was right. Within a year, I had quit all sports, and a year after that was getting into all kinds of mischief.

I think, aside from the coach's public humiliation, part of my reason for quitting that team was fear of failure. I've quit a lot of things in my life, not followed through on things, because of fear of failure. After all, if you quit, you can't fail. A twisted outlook, sure, but not uncommon.

I think I eventually overcame that fear. After high school, when I wanted something badly enough, I went for it, and I usually accomplished it. I went back to school at age 26 and graduated and got my degree. I wanted to go to work as a journalist, and I did that. Later, I wanted to become a schoolteacher, and I did that. Then, I wanted to go to Spain, and I did that. I wanted to write books and get them published, and I've done that.

We've all heard the stories about famous failures: NBA legend Michael Jordan, cut from his high school basketball team; best-selling author John Grisham, first novel rejected by sixteen agents and twelve publishing houses; Honda founder Soichiro Honda, turned down by Toyota for an engineering job after World War II; Walt Disney, fired by a newspaper editor for lacking in ideas; Thomas Edison, told by a teacher he was too stupid to learn and later invented the light bulb after more than 9,000 unsuccessful tries.

The only way to avoid failure is to never do anything. To avoid failure by never doing anything is to avoid life. To avoid living.

It's okay to fail. It's not okay to be a failure. If you fail, all that means is that you're trying. Trying is good, very good. Trying means you're living.

Take a chance. Go for your dreams.

Do at least one thing every day toward achieving your dreams, and every day is a success.

It's not the destination that counts. We all eventually reach the same destination. It's the journey that counts. Be true to yourself. Have a dream and work toward it each and every day. Let people love you, and love them back. All the rest is just life. It's just life...

"Remind yourself that it's okay not to be perfect."

Conclusion

Back in the olden days, when people spanked their kids—in my family, we got multiple lashings with a leather belt for various and sundry misdeeds—some parents supposedly used to say, "This is going to hurt me a lot worse than it hurts you," before they administered the disciplinary beating.

Well, writing this book just may have helped me a lot more than it helped you.

I can honestly say that about midway through the 30 days, my mindset began to change. Not in a major way, but I noticed little things. Learning to let things go, not dwell on the negativity that inevitably pushed its way into my mind. Learning to ignore those negative thoughts completely. Not give them an audience. Just like a kid who misbehaves looking for a reaction, ignore the behavior and it eventually stops. Ignore the negative thoughts, and they move on, perhaps looking for a more receptive audience somewhere else.

I have become a happier person over the past 30 days, and people have noticed the change. There is work left to do, but improvements have been made. I became a better person at work, and I no longer hate my job. *I no longer hate my job—wow.* The past few years, there have been times when I've absolutely hated my job to the point of despair. Most of the time, actually. I still can't say that I love my job, but I don't dread getting up in the morning and going to work anymore.

And here's the deal. Nothing about my job has changed. Everything there is still exactly the same. All the stress, all the ridiculous demands, the pressures, the thanklessness. None of that has changed one bit. What has changed is me, and my attitude.

That's amazing to me.

Several things happened these past 30 days that in the past would have thrown me right off the tracks. People and circumstances fell short of my lofty expectations. This is the type of thing that should have rocked my world, sent me spinning into disgust and disheartenment, wanting to throw my hands up and quit.

I didn't quit. I took it all in stride. Things are going to work out the way they're supposed to work out.

What a change.

So this stuff really does work. The important thing is consistency. Consistency is the key. Repetition. Practice. Over and over again.

You can't practice something once in a while and expect to make much progress, achieve any sort of mastery. People who achieve great things work hard. That's the bottom line for success

Hard work.

Bobby has seen his dreams come true. He didn't get there by just dreaming, wishing on a falling star, throwing a coin in a fountain or something. It took years and years—decades—of dedication and hard work. I saw some of it firsthand, so I know. He stumbled once in a while, and things looked bleak a time or two. But he hung in there. Kept dreaming and kept working. A little bit of luck here and there helped out, perhaps, but isn't luck said to be found at the intersection of hard work and opportunity?

Something like that, anyway.

Now, my challenge is to keep it going. Up my game. Continue to practice and work hard.

I've compiled some things at the end of this book that we all should do for the rest of our lives in order to continue growing and improving. Some helpful hints, suggestions, guidelines. They don't have to be done all at once, but at least some of them should be done every day.

There are ingredients for a gratitude list. Make one. Hang it in a prominent place, where you can't help but see it every day. The bathroom mirror. On the refrigerator. Somewhere. Look at it. Add to it. Look at it. Revise it. Look at it.

There is a list of practical ways to energize your life, and ways to relieve stress. Simple things you can do to feel better and improve your outlook. Try some. See what works for you.

And then I added a long list of affirmations, including those I used for my daily observations here, as well as others I found in various places. Pick your favorites, write them on note cards, and post them around your home. Take a few to work and post them there. Stick one or two in the sun visor of your vehicle. Carry some in your shirt pocket. Read them.

Like I said, if I can change, anyone can.

Try it.

It works.

Gratitude List

Here is a list of things for which anyone can be grateful. If you have these things, some of these things, any of these things, you're doing better than you think. Go ahead, grab some paper and pencil, and make your list.

Write down the things that are true for you. If you think of other things, add them.

You may be surprised at just how blessed you really are. Here we go:

You are alive.
You are healthy.
You can see.
You can hear.
You can speak.
You can walk.
You can read and write.
You have a roof over your head.
You have a nice pillow on your bed.
You have transportation.
You have clothes.
You have a job.
You have food and water.
You have enough money for the basics. Maybe more.
You have a family.
You have at least one good friend.

You have the freedom to do what you want.

There are seventeen things there for which to be grateful. How many do you have?

Hang on to your list. Stick it on the refrigerator (hey, there's another thing to be grateful for—you have a refrigerator!) and add things when you think of them. Look at your gratitude list. Be thankful for what you have. Develop an attitude of gratitude. It could change your life.

Ways to Energize Your Life

Practicing positive thinking and cultivating a more positive outlook on life is energizing, in and of itself. I can promise you that if you practice the principles in this book, you will have more energy throughout the day.

Feel better mentally and you will feel better physically, as well.

Negativity is energy draining; positivity is energy producing. And along with training yourself to think more positively, here are some simple and effective ways to further increase your energy levels naturally:

Stay on your feet at work.

Lots of jobs are sit-down jobs these days. Get away from your desk. Have a seat once in a while, when you have to or when you need a little break, but spend most of the day on your feet. Sitting down all day can cause a variety of unhealthy physical issues. Keep moving!

Get close to nature.

Go for a walk first thing in the morning. A wonderful, energizing way to start the day. Don't have time, you say? Too much to do in the morning to get ready for the day? Get up 30 minutes earlier. You can do it. Before you know it, getting up earlier will become part of your routine. Try it for one week, every day. Then try it for one more week.

Eat breakfast.

A big cup of coffee or an energy drink is not the way to start the day. Try blending a nice smoothie at night and put it in the refrigerator. Some almond milk, soy milk, or water, a cup or so of frozen or fresh fruit, throw in a banana, maybe an avocado, some kale or spinach, a couple of carrots, apple slices. Try different combinations of ingredients. Smoothies are a great breakfast.

Get enough sleep.

Quality sleep is a big issue for a lot of people, including me. Some recommended ways to promote better sleep include such things as making your sleeping quarters as dark as possible. No night light. Don't watch TV in the bedroom at bedtime. No phones, tablets, or computers. The light from these devices interferes with the body's natural sleep rhythms. Make sure your sleeping quarters are cool. Turn down the thermostat. Turn on the ceiling fan. Run a portable fan.

I have a little white noise machine that makes a fairly loud whirring noise to help drown out disruptive sounds, including a partner's snoring. Earplugs available at any drug store help produce a nice, quiet sleeping environment, as well.

Natural products like melatonin, magnesium supplements, and valerian root help with drowsiness and relaxation. I use these and they really work.

If you have serious fatigue during the day, maybe find yourself falling asleep in the afternoon or, worse, while you're driving home from work, you might have a sleep disorder that can be relieved or improved with help from a physician.

A number of years ago, I underwent an overnight sleep study, spending the night in a hospital sleep lab with electrodes and wires attached all over my body, and they discovered that restless leg syndrome was keeping me half-awake all night, never allowing me to enter the restorative stages of sleep. Now, I take medication for that and sleep much better. I know people who use those breathing masks at night and say it is life changing.

Meditation.

Great for calming and focusing the mind, learning to manage your thoughts. Not control your thoughts, but manage them, instead of them managing you. I like to fall asleep listening to meditation CDs using soft ear buds.

Sex.

Aside from the obvious fact that it feels good, sex has a number of benefits to mental and physical health. And I don't know about the rest of you, but after sex, I'm sure ready to roll over and go to sleep. A lot more fun than sleeping pills!

Journaling.

Keep a small notebook and pen or pencil beside the bed. Make a to-do list for the next day, so you won't lie there thinking about what needs to be done tomorrow. Spend a little time writing down your thoughts, whatever is on your mind. Get it off your mind and down on paper. It's amazing how much smaller problems seem when you look at them on paper.

~~~~~~

Simple Ways to Relieve Stress:

Deep breathing.

As simple as it sounds—and it works. Deep breaths from the abdomen (your middle should expand when you inhale and contract as you exhale) can clear the mind, slow the heart rate, and reduce blood pressure.

Meditation.

Also simple and effective. Sit or lie in a quiet place, in a chair or on the floor. Legs crossed or folded, leaning back against a chair or couch, if you wish. Close your eyes and breathe normally, in and out. Focus your mind on your breath only. Feel the air enter and exit your body. Try not to think about anything, just concentrate on your breath. When thoughts inevitably pop up—and they will—just let them pass on through. And they will. Refocus on the breath. Try five minutes at first, then ten minutes. Set a goal to meditate every day for two weeks and notice any results.

Get outside.

Nature gives off a healthy balance of negative and positive ions that help reduce stress. Take a long walk in the woods, the park, by a lake, or by the seashore. Sit and soak up some sunshine. Life is better outdoors. Get out of the house for a while.

Aromatherapy.

Various fragrances are designed to relieve stress and promote relaxation. Lavender oil, for example, can be used to help promote relaxation at bedtime and improve sleep quality.

Healing items.

Try things like crystals, one of those tabletop waterfall decorations, or large indoor plants. I wear a rather large positive energy pendant necklace that is supposed to attract positive energy. There are bracelets and other kinds of jewelry, as well. Do some research.

Hugs.

Hugs are a wonderful thing. A nice, warm embrace from someone you know or even from a stranger can make you feel better, reduce stress, ease tension, and brighten your day.

Massage.

A professional massage is a luxury for many of us, no doubt, but not only is a good rubdown an excellent way to relax and relieve stress, it also provides a number of important health benefits. If you've never had one, try it—you'll like it.

Epsom salts bath.

These are great. A hot bubble bath in itself is wonderful, but add some Epsom salts and get ready for a truly relaxing experience. The salt bath is said to draw toxins from the body, relieving stress and tension. Try adding a few drops of your favorite essential oil for even more healthy benefits.

Exercise classes.

Join the local gym or look for classes offered at the community center or other places. Exercise helps reduce stress, and working out with other people helps keep you motivated and energized.

Downsize and de-clutter.

In a nutshell, get rid of stuff. If you're like me and a lot of other people, you hang onto stuff way too long and for no good reason. Clutter is stressful. I know this for a fact because I've experienced it. Figure out what you really no longer need to hang onto and get rid of it. Take it to Goodwill. Go through your closet and get rid of the clothes you never wear any more.

What was it the comedian George Carlin said? "A house is just a place to keep your stuff while you go out and get more stuff." My wife wants to get a storage shed for the backyard. "For what?" I argue. It'll just be another place to put more stuff. If we have so much stuff inside our house that we need an extra place to put some of it, we have too much stuff.

Affirmations

Here is a list of positive affirmations gathered from various sources and found throughout this book.

- Be happy with what you have while working for what you want.
- There is always good for those who wish to see it.
- Stop waiting for things to happen. Go out and make them happen.
- You can't calm the storm. So stop trying. What you can do is calm yourself. The storm will pass.
- Everyone fails. The people who succeed are the ones who never stop trying.
- You have to learn a new way to think before you can master a new way to be.
- There is always something to be thankful for.
- Maybe the journey isn't so much about becoming anything. Maybe it's about unbecoming everything that isn't really you, so you can be who you were meant to be in the first place.
- Sometimes people with the worst past end up creating the best future.
- Live more; think less.
- Positive thinking makes a broken life beautiful.
- Happy people don't necessarily have the best of everything; they just make the best of everything that comes their way.

- Life is too short to worry about stupid things. Have fun. Regret nothing and don't let people bring you down.

- Growth can be painful. Change can be painful. But nothing is as painful as staying stuck.

- Things you are passionate about are not random—they are calling you.

- Don't get upset with people or situations; both are powerless without your reaction.

- When there is no turning back, we should concern ourselves only with the best way of going forward.

- The most important decision you make is to be in a good mood.

- Don't rush. Never settle. If it's meant to be, it will be.

- Maybe people point out what's wrong with you because they can't handle all that's right with you.

- The soul knows what to do to heal itself. The challenge is to silence the mind.

- People create their own storms, then get upset when it rains.

- What's on your mind becomes what's in your life. So think the thoughts you want to see.

- Instead of looking at what's depressing, look at what's a blessing.

- Forget what's gone, appreciate what still remains, and look forward to what's coming next.

- It all begins in your mind. What you think, you create.

- Change your mind; change your life.

- Don't ruin a good day by thinking about a bad yesterday.

- I am committed to being a better person today than I was yesterday. Better thoughts. Better actions. Better decisions.

- Your mind is a powerful thing. When you start to fill it with positive thoughts, your life will start to change.

- Make the rest of your life the best of your life.

- I'm learning to love myself, and it's the hardest thing I've ever done.

- Sometimes sand, water, sunshine, and good company are all you really need.

- I didn't do everything right, but I didn't do everything wrong, either.

- When there is no turning back, we should concern ourselves only with the best way of going forward.

- Just be happy. Don't let the stupid little things steal your happiness.

- A negative mind will never give you a positive life.

- Whatever your past, let go of it, and start a new, better beginning. You are open and ready to receive all that is good.

- The greatest weapon against stress is our ability to choose one thought over another.

- Life becomes easier when you let go of the unneeded stress. If it's out of your control, don't let it worry you.

- No matter how long we have traveled on the wrong road, we can always turn around.

- Do good things and good things will come your way.

- Surround yourself with people who make you happy.

- A river cuts through rock not because of its power, but because of its persistence. You can achieve anything you want as long as you keep trying.

- Be brave, even if you're not. Pretend. Nobody will know the difference.

- Fake it until you make it.

- It takes only one person to change your life. You.

- To be a star, you must shine your own light, follow your own path, and don't worry about the darkness, for that is when the stars shine brightest.

- Everything comes to you at the right time. Be patient and trust in the process.

A Small Favor to Ask

Thanks for reading this collection; I hope you found these stories meaningful or helpful in some way. If you did, please take just a moment to write a brief review of it on Amazon. Your reviews mean a great deal to me, and they help others find this book, so that more readers can read these stories and perhaps find some resonance with their own experience and answers of their own.

Get My Books FREE

Visit my website www.johnclarkbooks.com, and subscribe to my mailing list to get all of my new releases for free. I plan to write many books over the coming years, and I'd love to repay you for taking an interest in my work by allowing you to access all of my future work at no charge. When each new book is released, I'll send you an email with a link to the free book. No strings attached and nothing for sale ever. Subscribe today at www.johnclarkbooks.com

About the Author

 John Henry Clark III is an award-winning journalist, freelance writer, author and avid golfer who was born and raised in Texas. He grew up in northwest Houston playing sports at Oaks Dads Club and attending church with his parents, but decided as he got older that things he learned in Sunday school no longer made much sense.

Since then, he has spent a lifetime seeking answers and exploring a variety of beliefs. After a successful career as a newspaper reporter, Clark turned his lifetime love for learning into a new career as a public school teacher, and that gave him time during the summer months to pursue his project to research and write a book describing what people believe about God and why they believe what they believe.

That effort turned into the book, *Finding God: An Exploration of Spiritual Diversity in America's Heartland*. A tireless seeker, researcher and questioner, John has written a number of other fascinating books dealing with the human experience, from tragedies to triumphs and more, including *Camino: Laughter and Tears along Spain's 500-mile Camino de Santiago*. To read more of John's books, find answers to the meaning of life, and maybe discover something new about yourself, go here:
http://amzn.to/1EmgWa7

CPSIA information can be obtained
at www.ICGtesting.com
Printed in the USA
BVHW031303130821
614380BV00005B/126